Llandudno Travel Guide: Things to do in Llandudno

Llandudno Travel Guide: Things to do in Llandudno

A local's guide of things to do in Llandudno

Dylan Thomas

Table of contents

Introduction

Hello and thank you for choosing this guide to help you discover and enjoy all of the delights that Llandudno has to offer!

The aim of this guide is not to cover every single thing that Llandudno has to offer, but to focus on the things that I think are definitely worth exploring and enjoying.

The guide has been split into 3 sections:

Activities

Food & Drink

Accommodation

The best way to use this guide is to check the locations on the maps in each section and review how these align with the types of activities that you are looking for.

Whatever you are looking for, there is definitely something for you to enjoy in beautiful Llandudno.

Enjoy!

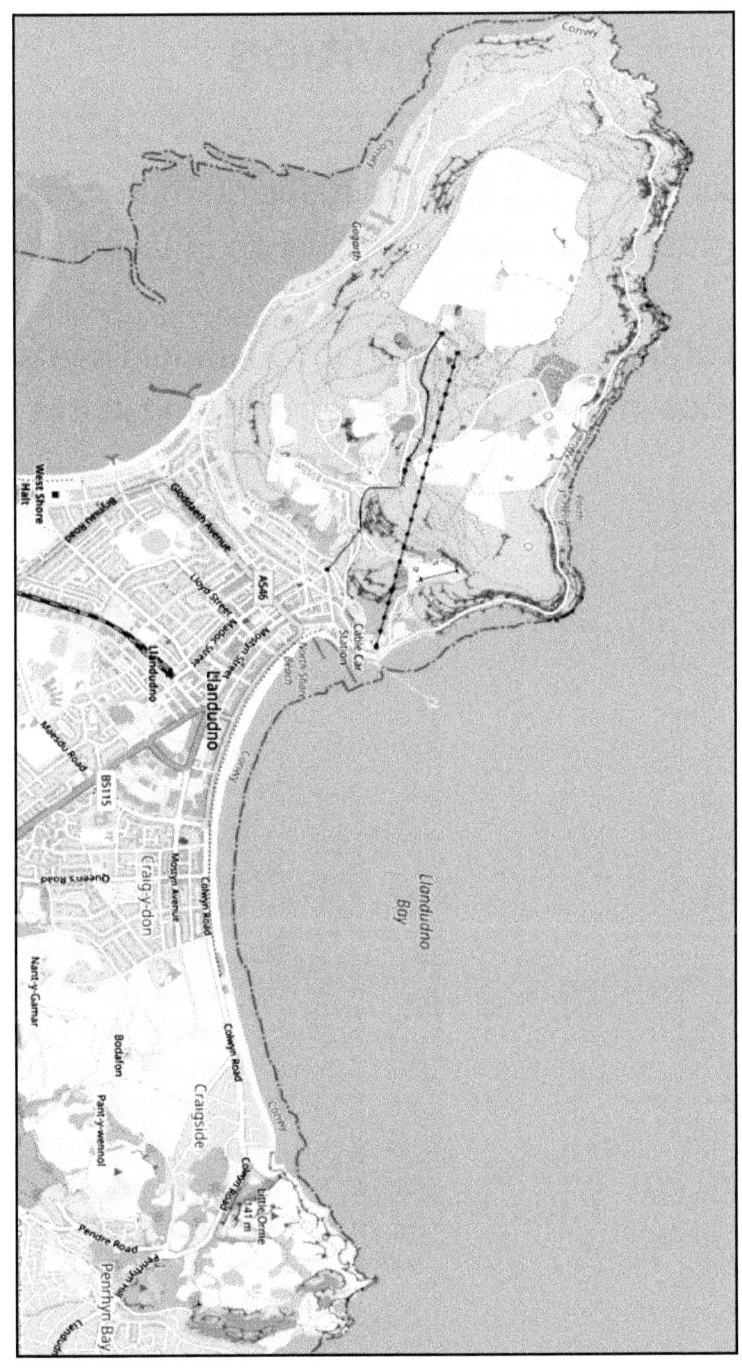
West Shore Halt
Gloddaeth Avenue
Lloyd Street
A546
Mostyn Street
Llandudno
Cable Car Station
North Shore Beach
Maesdu Road
B5115
Craig-y-don
Queen's Road
Mostyn Avenue
Colwyn Road
Llandudno Bay
Nant-y-Gamar
Bodafon
Pant-y-wennol
Craigside
Little Orme
141 m
Pendre Road
Penrhyn Bay
Gogarth
Conwy

Activities

This section of the book focuses on more active and sightseeing based things to do in Llandudno.

All of the great things that you should see and experience in Llandudno will be included in this section for everyone to enjoy.

Activities

Llandudno
Llandudno Bay
Craig-y-don
Craigside
Penrhyn Bay
Little Orme
141 m
West Shore Halt
Gloddaeth Avenue
Lloyd Street
Mostyn Avenue
Queen's Road
Colwyn Road
Maesdu Road
B5115
A546
Bodafon
Nant-y-Gamar
Pant-y-wennol
Pendre Road
Penrhyn Hill
1
2
3
4
5
6
7
8
9
10
11
12
13
14
15
16
17
18
19
20
21
22
23
24
25
26
27
28
29
30
31
32
33
34
35

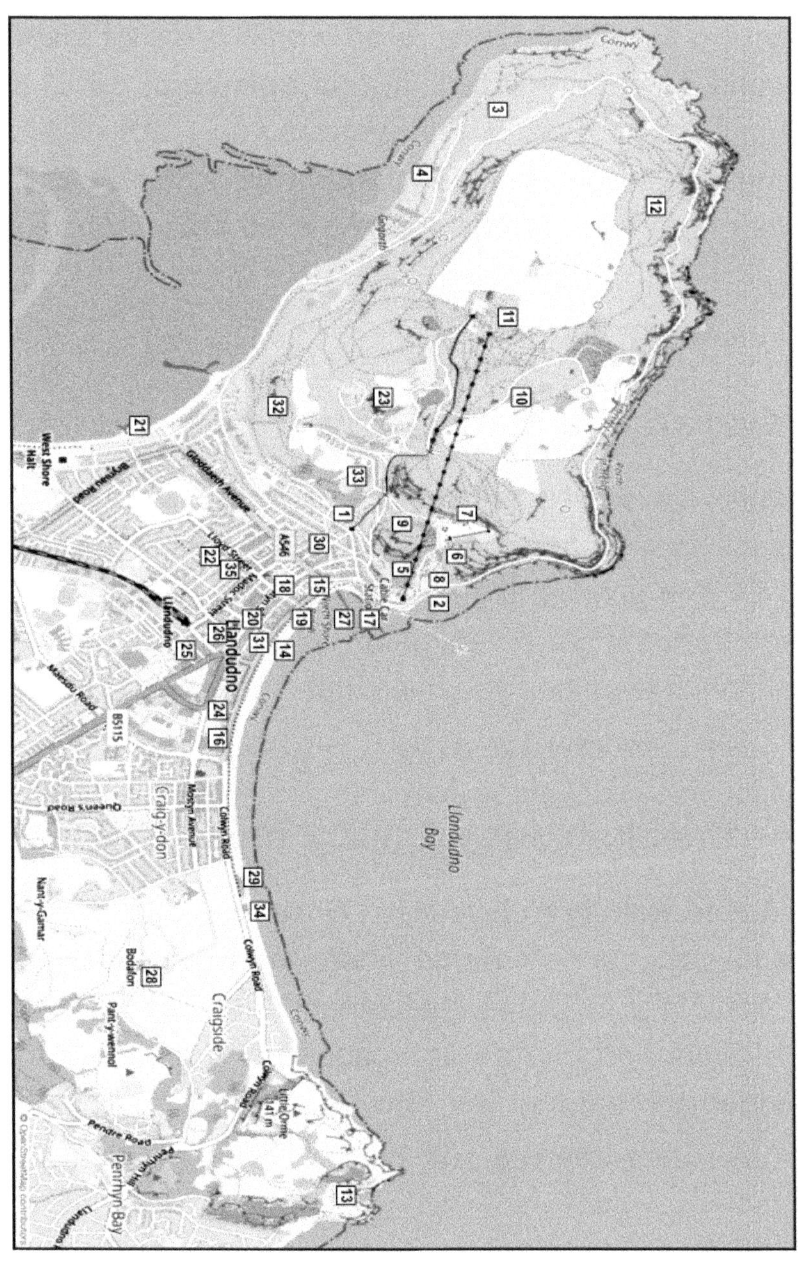

1. Take the tram up the Great Orme

The tram on the Great Orme is an iconic piece of Llandudno's history and can't be missed. It was opened in 1902 and has carried millions of passengers over the years. It's also the only remaining cable-operated street tramway in Great Britain. It's only open from late March to October so make sure you don't miss it.

GREATORMETRAMWAY.CO.UK

2. Travel around Marine Drive

The Marine Drive road around the Great Orme gives off some incredible views all times of the year. It's a toll road that costs around £4 in a car, but it's free to walk around. Make sure you approach from the correct direction as it is only a one way road! If you go in the evenings you can catch some amazing sunsets.

MARINE DRIVE, LLANDUDNO, LL30 2ND

3. See the old hidden artillery training range

Taking a nice walk from Llys Helig Drive, you can walk along to see the historic gunnery range where the Royal Artillery trained during World War 2. The range is abandoned but the build shells are still visible and can be approached and explored, normally quite hidden and not that well known!

END OF LLYS HELIG DRIVE, LL30 2XB

4. Wander down millionaires row

Llys Helig, mentioned in the Gunnery Range activity previously, also has the nickname 'Millionaire's Row'. This is because it's the most expensive street in Wales, with the average house price over £1 million. It's also a nice walk with multiple options to explore the Great Orme.

LLYS HELIG DRIVE, LL30 2XB

5. Take a ride on the cable cars

The cable cars on the Great Orme give off amazing panoramic views of the Bay of Llandudno, the Little Orme, the Conwy Estuary and miles out over the Irish Sea. The distance to the summit is just over a mile and the journey takes around nine minutes. Make sure to bring cash as they don't accept card payments.

WWW.LLANDUDNO.COM/LLANDUDNO-CABLE-CARS/

6. Travel down the Great Orme Toboggan

Take a ride the longest Cresta Toboggan run in Wales! At an amazing 575m long, you don't want to miss this great experience. Fantastic fun for all ages. It encircles the ski slope and gives off great views of the town of Llandudno whilst you fly down. You get two runs per ticket which is definitely enough fun to enjoy.

WWW.JNLLLANDUDNO.CO.UK/SLOPES/TUBING-TOBOGGANING/

7. Enjoy the Llandudno Snowsports Centre

The Snowsports Centre has a lot to offer for all, with mini golf available, skiing and snowboarding on the slope or even taking a rubber tube down the slope, there's something fun for all. The cafe just next door is also nice to enjoy.

WWW.JNLLLANDUDNO.CO.UK/SLOPES/TUBING-TOBOGGANING/

8. Wander through Happy Valley Gardens

Happy Valley is home to wildlife animals, plants and family walks. Happy Valley used to be a quarry stretching down the Great Orme. The quarry itself was donated as a gift from Lord Mostyn to the town of Llandudno when it was then developed into a garden. There is a nice open green area, along with a nice cafe and playground to enjoy. (Hint, there is also the elephant caves hidden nearby!)

HAPPY VALLEY, MARINE DRIVE, LLANDUDNO, DENBIGHSHIRE, LL30 2ND

9. Pen Dinas Witches Rocking Stone - Maen Sigl

Myth has it that witches would be tried on this stone to determine their guilt. If the stone rocked, they were innocent, but if it remained still, they were found guilty and executed. Whilst the stone does occasionally rock, it is really not very often... so the majority of the unfortunates who found themselves on trial were executed.

53.329220, -3.835082

10. Walk around the park wall

There is a lovely walk around the summit of the Great Orme, mostly known to locals, but gives off great views of all of the surrounding areas. You can park for free just above St Tudno's Church, and walk around the wall until you end up back at the summit. Take some layers as it does get quite windy!

WWW.CONWY.GOV.UK/EN/RESIDENT/LEISURE-SPORT-AND-HEALTH/COAST-AND-COUNTRYSIDE/ASSETS/DOCUMENTS/GREAT-ORME-NATURE-TRAILS.PDF

11. Mini golf at the summit

The summit of the Great Orme has a great mini golf course that overlooks North Wales. It's only around £5 per person and is open March to November. It's an 18 hole course, with a spectacular view.

WWW.VISITCONWY.ORG.UK/THINGS-TO-DO/ROCKY-PINES-ADVENTURE-GOLF-P275331

12. Watch the goats

Llandudno became famous around the world during the Covid lockdowns, when the goats came back into the town and took over! These goats already have a name for themselves as a ranking soldier of the Royal Welsh Battalion.

ANYWHERE ON THE GREAT ORME!

13. See the seals at the Little Orme and Angel bay

The Great Orme has a little brother, the Little Orme, sat on the side closest to Penrhyn Bay. It provides a lovely view over Llandudno from a different view than most see. You can park for free in Penrhyn Beach and walk to Angel Bay and maybe catch a glimpse of the seals from a safe distance! You can also follow the path to the top of the headland for a great view.

116 PENRHYN BEACH E, PENRHYN BAY, LLANDUDNO LL30 3RW

14. Walk along the promenade

The promenade on Llandudno is an iconic part of this town built in 1884, and definitely can't be missed to walk down! It's quite a long walk down and back at 4 miles, but you don't need to walk it all. I'd also recommend sitting on the benches and people watching, it's always a good laugh!

WWW.LLANDUDNO.COM/PLACE/LLANDUDNO-PROMENADE/

15. Watch the 1860s Puppet Show Punch & Judy

In 1860, Richard Codman, a travelling showman, was stranded in Llandudno after his horse died. He collected driftwood from the beach and hand carved the Punch & Judy puppets, which are still in use today. The show is now in the hands of the Codman family's fifth generation. Punch & Judy is a traditional Victorian-style show that features all of the old characters and slapstick comedy.

N PARADE, LLANDUDNO LL30 2LP

16. Catch a show in Venue Cymru

While in North Wales, why not try to catch a show in Llandudno? There are a variety of shows on, such as a comedian, a rock music show, a theatre performance, or even a family workshop to get the whole family creative. Check out the website to see what's going on during your visit.

WWW.VENUECYMRU.CO.UK

17. Llandudno pier

Few things say "seaside holiday" like a stroll along the pier, and Llandudno Pier is a true gem! It's a traditional seaside pier from the late 1800s with an array of shops, cafes, bars, and attractions – fun for the whole family! It's a Grade II listed traditional seaside pier from the late 1800s with an array of shops, cafes, bars, and attractions – fun for the whole family!

LLANDUDNOPIER.COM

18. Shops on Mostyn Street

Mostyn Street is Llandudno's main thoroughfare. It runs parallel to the promenade road behind it and is nearly as long as the promenade itself. It extends from the top of town near the Empire Hotel all the way down to the bottom of town near Mostyn Broadway. Mostyn Street is home to a variety of shops and cafes, each of which offers its unique set of services.

MOSTYN STREET, LLANDUDNO, WALES, LL30 2PS

19. Donkey rides on Llandudno

Why not visit Llandudno's North Shore beach, where children can enjoy the experience and thrill of donkey rides during the summer holidays, while parents can chat and be made welcome by the friendly and local proprietor? Open during summer season and some school holidays. Weather permitting.

VISITCONWY.ORG.UK/THINGS-TO-DO/NORTH-SHORE-DONKEY-RIDES-P305891

20. Follow the Alice in Wonderland trail!

Explore Llandudno while learning about Alice Liddell (the real Alice in Wonderland), who lived in the resort in the 1860s. Starting at the Tourist Information Centre and using the map you can buy there as a guide, walk around the trail following the 55 bronze cast Rabbit footprints. Discover a plethora of Alice in Wonderland sculptures dotted around the town for a fun day out. The tour takes you past the Town Hall, down Madoc Street, past the shops and galleries, onto the Prom, and into Happy Valley.

HTTPS://WWW.VISITWALES.COM/THINGS-DO/CULTURE/CULTURAL-ATTRACTIONS/ALICE-WONDERLAND-TOUR-LLANDUDNO

21. West Shore beach sunset

Make sure you catch the sunset at the West Shore Llandudno beach, which gives off amazing views at all times of the day, but especially at sunset. Be careful if you head out onto the beach as the tide turns very quick and catches lots of people out!

LLANDUDNO, LL30 2BB

22. Boathouse Climbing Centre

Situated in the old RNLI lifeboat station, the Boathouse Climbing Centre offers a welcoming space for all ages and abilities. Many features have been retained and have even been incorporated into this new era for the Boathouse. The original stone work that can be found in the Climbing Tower forms part of the climbing routes, bringing a little bit of the outdoors, inside.

BOATHOUSECLIMBINGCENTRE.CO.UK

23. Great Orme Copper Mine

A visit to Great Orme Mines is a thought-provoking and educational experience that children and adults of all ages can enjoy. Walking through tunnels mined over 3,500 years ago gives visitors a sense of the harsh conditions our prehistoric forefathers faced in their quest for copper. Return to the surface by following the paths that lead around the surface excavations. View the opencast mine, learn how our forefathers converted rock into metal at the smelting shelter, and peer down the 145-meter-deep Victorian mine shaft.

WWW.GREATORMEMINES.INFO

24. Swim in Llandudno Swimming pool

Llandudno Swimming Centre has a variety of facilities to offer, including a Main Pool, a Training Pool, and a Fitness Suite. Llandudno Swimming Centre offers a variety of activities that allow you to stay fit and healthy while having fun.

WWW.VISITCONWY.ORG.UK/THINGS-TO-DO/LLANDUDNO-SWIMMING-CENTRE-P275601

25. Admire some Modern Art

MOSTYN, Wales' largest modern art gallery, is housed behind a traditional Edwardian façade. Six galleries housed in traditional rooms mixed with beautiful modern construction feature frequently changing exhibitions by artists and craftspeople from Wales and throughout the world. There's something for everyone here, with pleasant employees, activities for all ages, a great shop, and a bright and airy café with views of the sea. The building is fully accessible, and entrance is FREE.

WWW.MOSTYN.ORG

26. Try some choccies at the Chocolate museum

At the Llandudno Chocolate Experience, you will learn about the history of chocolate. There are nine eras to explore, with plenty of chocolate samples to enjoy as you go. The videos will accompany you on your chocolatey adventure, beginning in the Maya forests and ending in the twentieth century... The attraction is jam-packed with information and activities for kids. There is also a working artisan chocolate studio where you can observe the chocolatiers at work.

LLANDUDNOCHOCOLATEEXPERIENCE.CO.UK

27. Llandudno boat trips

Never fear, even if you're just visiting Llandudno for a short time, you may take advantage of the fantastic small scale excursions that depart directly from the promenade's jetty. Boats travel to spectacular destinations such as the Great Orme, the Little Orme, the Wind Turbines, and more. Board the Seajay or any of the other boats that may be anchored and ready to leave. Trips run throughout the day, so you can select one that works for you. Trips are available everyday, weather permitting, from April 1st to October 31st.

VISITCONWY.ORG.UK/THINGS-TO-DO/LLANDUDNO-BOAT-TRIPS-P277291

28. Bodafon farm

Bodafon Farm Park is a working farm which also lets you get up close and personal with the animals. There's something for everyone, from tiny Pygmy Owls to massive Shire horses. Meet the Shires family in a beautiful location between Llandudno and The Little Orme. Most days, you may see the horses, either at their stables where guests can meet them "face to face," training in one of the fields, or out and about on the farm.

BODAFONFARMPARK.COM

29. Paddling pool

This is one of Wales' largest outdoor paddling pools. It is particularly popular throughout the summer season and measures 116m - 21m with a maximum depth of 2ft / 0.6m. Ridiculously Rich by Alana, the Apprentice Winner, is right next to the pool! The promenade and adjacent areas have limited free parking, so arrive early to prevent disappointment.

COLWYN RD, LLANDUDNO LL30 3AA

30. Bonkerz fun centre

Bonkerz Fun Centre is so much more than your average soft play centre, it offers a completely unique experience with its cutting edge soft play facilities and unique Medieval Castle themed environment, plus boasting comfortable seating and excellent quality cafe for parents to lounge in.

BONKERZFUNCENTRE.CO.UK

31. St John's Church

St John's is located in the heart of Llandudno's town centre, on the main retail strip, just a short walk from the seafront and hotels. It was created to meet the needs of both tourists and locals, and it still has a reputation for sound preaching, excellent singing, and a friendly welcome. In the name of Christ, their mission in the heart of Llandudno is welcome and sanctuary. The regular exhibitions and male voice choir concerts are a well-known and anticipated element of the Llandudno visitor offering.

53-55 MOSTYN ST, LLANDUDNO LL30 2NN

32. Haulfre gardens

Haulfre Gardens is a short walk that runs right across the face of the Great Orme, providing spectacular views of Llandudno and the Conwy Mountains. Along the way, you'll gain access to the Zig Zag path that leads to the summit of the Orme, as well as wildlife and a small cafe with a variety of food and drink. A wonderful walk across the face of the Great Orme leads to Haulfre Gardens. Although it may appear tricky and dangerous, a safe and sufficient path has been constructed using tarmac to assure a safe and accident-free walk.

CWLACH RD, LLANDUDNO LL30 2HT

33. Test your skills on the Great Orme Golf Course

Now don't be put off, this Golf Course is a great mix between mini-golf and a real golf course. I've never played golf before and this is always a good laugh! The owners are very friendly, and the course is sat on the side of a big hill, which definitely adds a layer of difficulty when your ball rolls away! It's much less well known about so you'll be able to avoid the crowds!

WWW.GREATORMEGOLFCOURSE.WALES

34. RNLI Lifeboat Station

The functioning Llandudno Lifeboat Station is open to the public for tours. A viewing gallery overlooks the lifeboats, as well as an exhibition detailing the RNLI's and Llandudno Lifeboat Station's history from the beginning to the present day. The lifeboats and launch equipment are described in detail in the viewing gallery. Records of Llandudno lifeboat rescues from 1861 to the present can be found on the opposite walls. A History Wall, as well as active audio and video rescue clips, may be found in the Visitor Experience Room. There's also an interactive 'Photo-me' machine with a selection of crew images to highlight your face, as well as an area with 'Crew Kit' for kids to try on.

RNLI.ORG/FIND-MY-NEAREST/LIFEBOAT-STATIONS/LLANDUDNO-LIFEBOAT-STATION

35. Penderyn Whiskey Distillery Tour

Since 1999, Penderyn has been producing award-winning single malt whiskies and spirits at their Brecon Beacons distillery. Since then, the distillery has grown and now exports to countries all over the world. The latest addition is the Penderyn Lloyd Street facility, which is situated in Llandudno's Old Board School and opened in May 2021 with a shop, tourist centre, and distillery. Tours of the distillery are provided to witness how the whiskey is manufactured, as well as tastings.

WWW.PENDERYN.WALES/LLANDUDNO/

Food & Drink

With lots of places to eat and drink in Llandudno, there's no I could ever fit them all into this small guide! In which case, I have hand picked a few of my favourites that you should try.

There are plenty of restaurant specific guides online which will go into unbelievable detail about your specific area which are definitely worth exploring if you have the time.

However, if you're looking for my local recommendations, then look no further than this next section.

Map - Food & drink

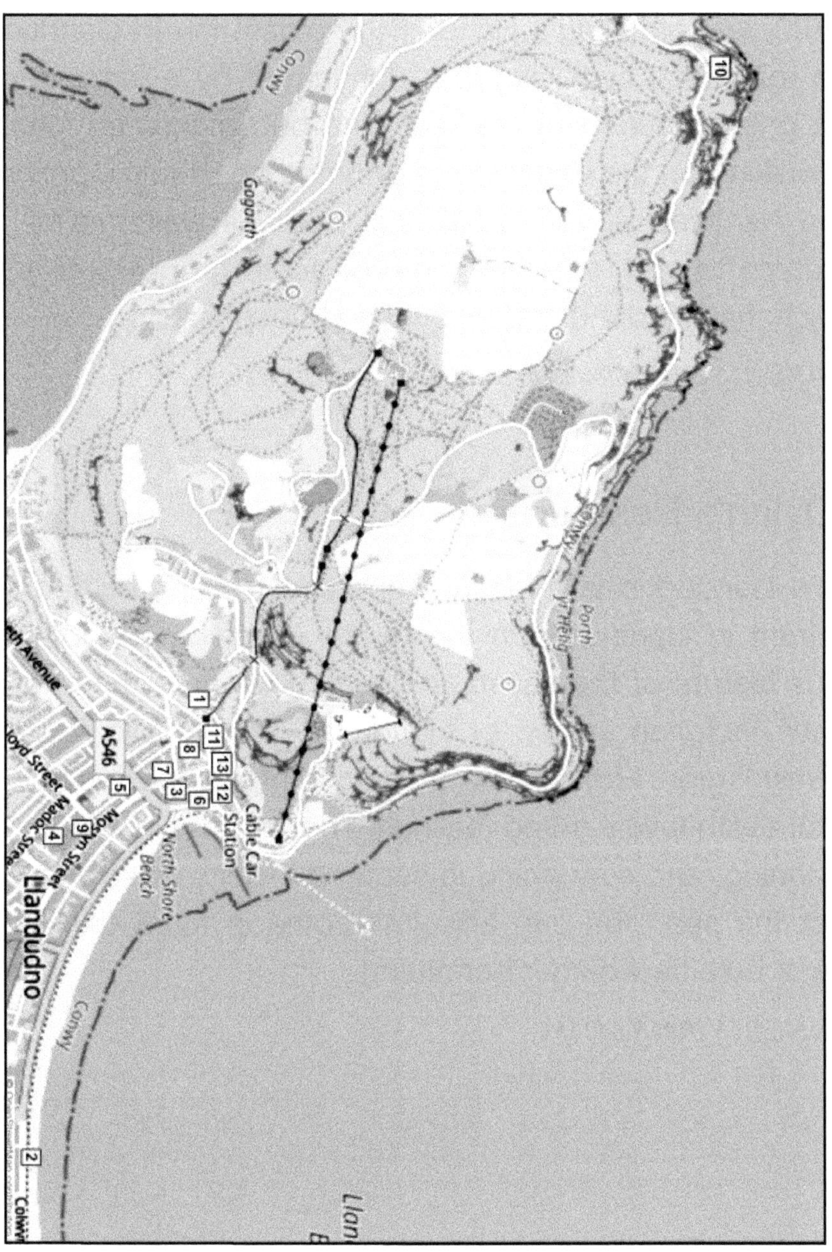

1. Kings Head Pub

The 300-year-old King's Head is the oldest inn in Llandudno. It has a traditional split level bar dominated by a large open fire and a grill restaurant at the rear. The pub makes an ideal stop after walking on the Great Orme or riding on Britain's only cable-hauled tramway. A very traditional pub will welcome all those who come to visit, whether it be for some proper pub grub, or simply to have a drink and enjoy the atmosphere.

RESTAURANTGURU.COM/KINGS-HEAD-LLANDUDNO

2. Dylan’s Restaurant

Dylan's Llandudno is a family-friendly restaurant located on the waterfront in Llandudno in the former Washington Hotel. It's a famous feature of the seashore, located towards the end of the majestic Victorian sweep of Llandudno promenade & bay. The old Washington Hotel, now a restaurant, is a Grade II listed structure with lovely grand feelings. The award-winning cuisine is outstanding, and everything is sourced locally, whether from the hills or the sea. You can also just come in for a drink and sit inside or outside weather permitting.

DYLANSRESTAURANT.CO.UK

3. Johnny Dough's Wood-Fired Pizza

Started in 2016 by a 38-year-old geologist from Llandudno working in Ethiopia for a Canadian mining corporation (very random I know!), Johnny Dough's Wood-Fired Pizza has been providing amazing pizza ever since. The new restaurant hit the ground running with an expanded menu that included some local twists like Great Orme Goat's Cheese, Menai Strait Mussels Marinière, and Anglesey Sheep Shish Kebab and quickly became a local favourite as well as a welcome addition to the town's tourism sector.

JOHNNYDOUGHS.COM

4. TAPPS Micropub

Interested in excellent beers and ciders, from IPAs to Lagers to Pale Ales? This is the place for you. Situated on Madoc Street, the Micropub looks unassuming from the outside, but the friendly welcoming staff will be happy to help find you a drink that you'll definitely enjoy. It's quite small so sometimes you have to chance it to find a seat, but the seats do wrap round the back. They have board games and chess sets as well to help you enjoy your time there.

TAPPS MICROPUB, 35 MADOC ST, LLANDUDNO LL30 2TL

5. The Cottage Loaf Pub

Llandudno's Cottage Loaf, arguably the best pub for food in the area, is located down a quiet street off the town's main drag. Of course, there's more to it than just a gorgeous setting, as this old gem offers up some seriously delicious pub grub. A broad range of light snacks are offered, as well as some heartier options, like as a Steak and Conwy pie that is as delicious as it gets. All of the desserts are also made from scratch.

THE-COTTAGELOAF.CO.UK

6. Osbourne House Restaurant

Osborne House, a sumptuously restored Victorian mansion near Llandudno's seafront, epitomises old-school opulence, with enormous rooms stretching the length of the structure, a profusion of rich fabrics, and Roman-style columns. Instead of contemporary minimalism, Osborne's Café & Grill is a riot of luxurious curtains, flashing crystal chandeliers, gilt-edged mirrors, and original canvases. It's a romantic – but relaxed – setting for all-day dining with an eclectic modern twist. The food here is superb and is probably priced a bit higher than your average pub, but it's also a bit fancier!

OSBORNEHOUSE.CO.UK

7. Providero Coffee

Looking for some of the best coffee in Llandudno, in my opinion this is where you'll find it! Sat at the top of Mostyn Street towards the Great Orme, this coffee shop also has some beautiful cakes and sandwiches available as well. If you go in and don't see any seating available, don't worry as you can either sit outside, or next door in the large room where the the bike hire shop is located at the back.

PROVIDERO FINE TEA AND COFFEES, 112 MOSTYN ST, LLANDUDNO LL30 2SW

8. The Snowdon Pub

The Snowdon is a typical pub in every sense of the term, tucked away on a quiet Llandudno backstreet. It is one of the area's oldest bars, dating back to the early 1800s when Llandudno was a little mining settlement on the Great Orme with only a few people dreaming of what the town may become. The bar is located just above town, at the end of a delightful Victorian terrace that you've probably passed on your route up to the Great Orme Tramway. For many years, the tavern has been a firm favourite of locals and travellers who have enjoyed frequenting it.

THESNOWDON.CO.UK

9. The Ham Bone Café

Llandudno has a fantastic deli-café that serves a wide variety of cuisine all day. Freshly cooked sandwiches are one alternative, which are ideal for a picnic on the Promenade. Breakfast is available until 11:30 a.m, or come in for lunch for burgers, fishcakes, steak-and-ale pies, big pizzas, and a constantly changing menu of specials. Check the hours of opening, however during the summer, it stays open later in the evening to take advantage of the lighter evenings.

THEHAMBONE.CO.UK

10. Rest and Be Thankful Café

On the Great Orme in Llandudno, North Wales, you'll find the Rest and Be Thankful Cafe. It's a popular stop for walkers climbing the Great Orme because it's at the highest point and, in fact, the half-way point on the Marine Drive. It is the only cafe on the Marine Drive and offers good quality and value, as well as beautiful views of Anglesey, Puffin Island, and the Isle of Man on a clear day. If you take a walk around Marine Drive, this is a definite place that you will be grateful for.

RESTANDBETHANKFUL.NET

11. Fish Tram Chips

This is where the locals flock for good-value fish lunches, either to take away or to sit in the small dining room, because it consistently serves out great, fresh fish and handmade side dishes with unaffected warmth. Probably the best deal in Llandudno; summer hours are extended. If you carry your food down to the promenade, be aware that you may be harassed by seagulls who seem to be able to smell fish and chips from miles away. Feeding them will only make things worse!

FISH TRAM CHIPS, 24 OLD RD, LLANDUDNO LL30 2NB

12. The Seahorse Restaurant

If you enjoy fresh fish, this is the place to be. Don, the chef at Llandudno's only dedicated seafood restaurant, is a keen fisherman, and the menu reflects his passion for the local catch: Menai mussels in white wine, or Thai crab fishcakes with pickled cucumber. The restaurant is a split-level affair: upstairs is decorated with large Mediterranean murals, while the more intimate cellar room has a cosier feel.

THE-SEAHORSE.CO.UK

13. Snooze Bar

Snooze is a fantastic find, offering a great selection of food and drink in a bustling upmarket setting where smart clothing is the norm. If you really want to go all out, you can stay in one of the four luxury boutique guest rooms for a night or longer. Diners can choose from a variety of huge sharing platters that are perfect for two or more people. Smaller sharing plates, stone-baked gourmet pizzas, and a select dessert menu are also available, including a combination of desserts, which combines three of the best desserts currently on the menu on one plate.

SNOOZEWINEBAR.COM

Continues on next page...

Accommodation

Although I'm not necessarily an expert to staying in hotels and B&Bs in Llandudno, I've still heard of recommendations from friends and family.

In this section, I have named a small selection of places to stay that I would choose to stay in if I was staying over in Llandudno.

This section will be a bit lighter compared to others because of this, but I hope you will still find this useful!

Map - Accommodation

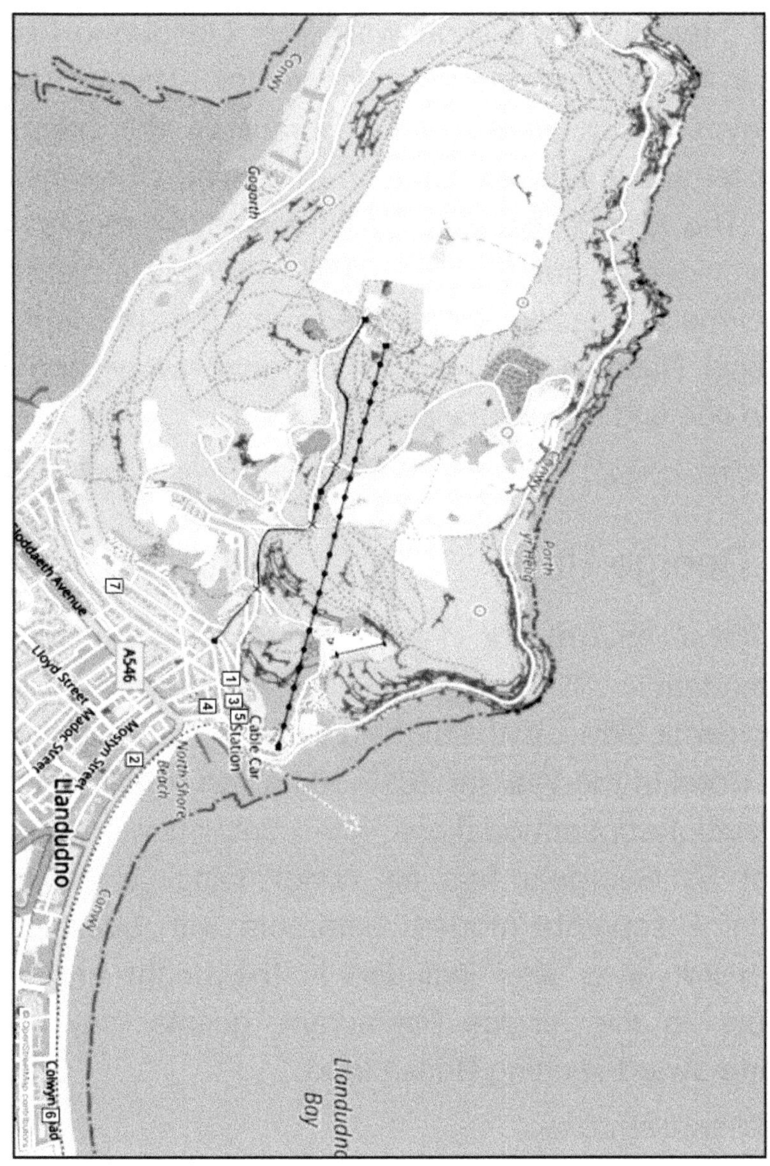

1. Empire Hotel

The Empire Hotel & Spa has a sauna, an indoor pool, and free wireless internet. It is a short walk from Llandudno Pier and is located in the area's famed nightlife sector. This Victorian hotel has a gym, a sun deck, and a library on the premises. An outdoor terrace is a lovely location to unwind when the weather is nice. The Empire Hotel & Spa features 54 rooms, each of which provides a variety of amenities to ensure a pleasant stay. Great Orme is easily accessible from the accommodation. Snowdonia National Park is a short drive away, and there is plenty to see and do in the vicinity.

EMPIREHOTEL.CO.UK

2. St George Hotel

The beach is only a 1-minute walk away from this accommodation. St George's Hotel is located next to the majestic Great Orme, with stunning views across Llandudno Bay. The AA Hotel of the Year for 2015-16 has an excellent restaurant and beautiful accommodations with complimentary WiFi. Each room at St George's has air conditioning, a desk, and a television. A separate modern bathroom with quality products and a hairdryer is also included in the bright and spacious bedrooms. In the Terrace Restaurant, guests may enjoy sea vistas and award-winning British food.

STGEORGESWALES.CO.UK

3. Snooze

As mentioned in the Food & Drink section, Snooze is a newly refurbished upmarket Llandudno Wine Bar with B&B Rooms, their menu has been developed with a passion for serving fresh and tasteful sharing platters and stone baked pizza's. The bar offers a wide selection of quality wines and local beers. Situated at the foot of the Great Orme on the Golden Mile and close to many exciting North Wales activities. Snooze is 200 meters away from the Pier, Tram Station and the main shopping High Street.

SNOOZEWINEBAR.COM/ROOMS

4. Osbourne House

This small hotel on the promenade is furnished with 'impressive grandeur,' with splendid public rooms decorated with oil paintings and gilded mirrors; on the upper floors, most of the 'characterful' suites overlook the sea. The Maddocks and Waddy families, Llandudno hoteliers who have been at the helm of sister hotel The Empire since 1946, have owned the hotel for more than 20 years. Each well-appointed suite contains a sitting area, marble bathroom, and a working gas fireplace; continental breakfasts are served in the room. The 'ornate' Victorian dining room has a brasserie-style meal; guests can also eat, swim, and use the sauna at The Empire, which is 200 yards away.

OSBORNEHOUSE.CO.UK

5. Belmont Hotel

The Belmont Llandudno is a brand-new boutique hotel on the Promenade in this spectacular North Wales resort. The hotel has elegant, stylish rooms, many of which have views of Llandudno Bay. Check-in, unwind, splurge, and get away. Located near the Llandudno Pier at the top of town. Originally constructed in the 1850s. The Belmont Llandudno is one of the Parade's oldest structures.

EVERBRIGHTGROUPHOTELS.COM/BELMONTHOTEL

6. Grafton Hotel

For the best pricing, they recommend contacting directly. The Grafton is a Grade II listed building with a 4* rating that dates back to the 1860s. They are a family-run business located on the promenade in Llandudno, a historic Victorian seaside resort. They provide a variety of rooms to choose from (doubles, twins, family, ground floor and sought after, interconnecting family suites). All of the rooms have modern en-suite bathrooms. Many accommodations have breathtaking views of the sea and the Ormes, while others have distant mountain views. A complimentary substantial full cooked breakfast (lighter choices available) will be served in their lovely sea view breakfast room during your stay.

THEGRAFTONHOTEL.COM

7. Abbey House B&B

Contemporary B&B in an Old Victorian House. They say that they treat all their guests as 'friends still to be made'. Whether you have selected them to be your partners in creating that perfect weekend away, or need a special place to 'stay over' whilst on business in the area they are there to make your stay as enjoyable as they possibly can.

ABBEYHOUSE.CYMRU

End of guide

Thank you for reading, I hope you found the guide useful for you and I hope that your time in Llandudno is something that you enjoy.

Author Bio

Dylan Thomas, although sharing the name with the famous poet, is unfortunately not a poet, but certainly enjoys writing! Raised in Llandudno, North Wales, he has created this guide to help all visitors to the region. He has spent decades enjoying the Welsh countryside and visiting the best that North Wales has to offer. Hopefully this transfers well to a locally written guide for those who want to come and enjoy the region.

www.ingramcontent.com/pod-product-compliance
Ingram Content Group UK Ltd.
Pitfield, Milton Keynes, MK11 3LW, UK
UKHW022009190726
13853UKWH00004B/1824

9 798809 890151